Article 9

Article 9 applies to transactions, regardless of its form, that creates a security interest in personal property or fixtures by contract; agricultural lien; sale of accounts; chattel paper, payment intangibles, promissory notes; consignment

A-A-P-P- Does Art 9 apply? Attached? Perfection? Priority?

Classification of Collateral

Debtor's use controls classification (with exception of farm products)

Goods- All things that are movable when a security interest attaches

Consumer Goods- Goods used or bought primarily for personal, family or household purposes.

Inventory- - Most common if held for sale by business. Goods other than farm products held for sale or lease, raw materials, work in progress or materials consumed in business.

Equipment-(catchall)- Goods other than farm products, consumer goods or inventory.

Farm Products- Crops, livestock, or supplies used/consumer in farming operation; or products of crops/livestock in their unmanufactured state.

Process

Attachment- 1. Value must be given (i.e. loan); 2. Debtor must have rights in the collateral; and 3. Secured party must take possession of the collateral or the debtor must authenticate a security agreement containing a description of the collateral.

- **Value-** usually by loan
- **Rights-** business has rights in its equipment
- **Authenticate-** sign

Perfection- A security interest is perfected when it has attached and when any additional steps required for perfection have occurred. Either: 1. Possession of the collateral by the secured party or 2. Filing of a financing statement with respect to the collateral.

- **Ways:** 1. Filing appropriate paperwork (UCC 1) at appropriate location (can be done before Security agreement signed)
- **2.** Secured party takes possession of collateral
- 3. Secured Party taking control of the property
- 4. Automatic perfection

Financing Statement- Document that gives notice of creditor's interest in debtors property. (UCC 1)

- **Contents-** 1. Name of debtor; 2. Name of secured party (or it's rep); 3. Description of the collateral
- **Description-** will be sufficient if it ID's by type of property
- **Financing statement may be filed before security interest granted**

After-Acquired Property Clause- Security Interest created in collateral that debtor does not own at the time of filing but acquires in the future. Allows debtor to encumber property s/he doesn't own at the time of the secured transaction.

Proceeds: EX: Security interest in bikes & debtor acquires computer for trading bike for it.

- Because the computer was acquired upon the exchange of the collateral, the computer is proceeds of that collateral
- A security interest in collateral extends to the identifiable proceeds of that collateral.
- If security interest in bikes perfected, the security interest in computer is perfected because the security interest in the original collateral was perfected by the filing of a financing statement in the same office where a financing statement would have been filed to perfect a security interest in the computer

PMSI Consumer Goods (AUTOMATIC PERFECTION)- A PMSI in consumer goods arises when the secured party advances $ or credit to enable to debtor to acquire the consumer goods.

Sale of Collateral by Debtor- A security interest continues in collateral even after a sale or other disposition of that collateral, unless the creditor authorized that disposition free of the security interest or another Article 9 exception applied.

UCC 9-317(B)- Buyers who give value and receive delivery of goods without knowledge of an unperfected security interest in the goods.

- Must purchase from person in the business of selling the goods

9-320(A)(B)- BORC- A buyer in the ordinary course if a person that buys goods in Good faith, without knowledge that the sale violates the rights of another person in the goods and bought in the ordinary course of a person in business of selling goods of that kind.

- Good faith- Consumer acts in a manner consistent with reasonable commercial standards of fair dealing
- Buyer in ordinary course from a person who used the goods for personal, family or household purposes takes free of a perfected security interest if: 1. The buyer had no knowledge of the security interest; 2. The buyer gave value for the goods; and 3. The buyer purchased the goods primarily for personal/family or household purposes; and 4. Purchase occurred before the filing of a financing statement covering the goods
- **Won't be BORC IF-** 1st time seller has sold this type of good
- **IF found not to be BORC-** Security interest continues even after equipment sold to buyer

Priority/ Remedies

Basic Rule- "First in time" Conflicting Security Interests will rank according to priority in time of filing or perfection

PMSI- Perfected PMSI in goods other than livestock has priority over conflicting security interest in same goods if PMSI is perfected at time debtor receives possession of the collateral or within 20 days.

BORC- Takes free of Security interests in created by seller even though perfected and even though buyer knows of its existence.

- **Requires:** 1. Must buy in good faith; 2. Must not know sale is in violation of security agreement; 3. Must be in ordinary course of seller; 4. Must buy from one who is in business of selling those kinds of goods.

Default- Conditions that constitute default are determined by provisions in security agreement, or if no definition in security agreement, upon non-payment by debtor. Other examples include: non-insurance of collateral, debtor's removal of collateral, loss/destruction of collateral, debtor's bankruptcy.

Repossession- Self-help remedy as long as no 'breach of the peace can result'.

Foreclosure sale- A secured party must send reasonable notification to certain persons. Includes: debtor, any secondary obligor. Disposition of the collateral must be done in a commercially reasonable manner. (method/time/place/manner and terms)

- **Notice-** Must be sent more than 10 days before the auction and state the date/method of the disposition

Deficiency- If after disposition of collateral, there is amount owed to secured creditor. Debtor liable for secured party for deficiency.

Disabling-If the collateral is large/heavy equipment, secured party allowed to render equipment unusual and dispose of on debtor's premises rather than removing.

Conflict of Laws/Civil Procedure

Conflict of Laws- Is the part of the law of each state which determines what effect is given to fact that case might have a relationship with more than one state. Court must determine which states law should govern the controversy.

Corporation: By statute, a corporation is a resident both where it is incorporated and where it has its principal place of business.

- Some courts use a nerve center test that focuses on where the corporations decision making authority was located. Other courts use a corporate-activities/operating-assets test that focused on where a corps business activities occur
- **HERTZ-** Supreme Court decided that a corporations principal place of business for diversity purpose would be deemed to be 'the place where its officers direct, control and coordinate corp activities' i.e. nerve center

<u>Choice of Law Forum Clause-</u> Parties agreement as to place of an action cannot oust a state that has proper Personal Jurisdiction, but such an agreement will be given effect unless unfair/unreasonable.

<u>Venue:</u> Refers to the proper judicial district in which to bring the action. The venue should be a convenient place to try the case based on the location of the witnesses, the evidence or the like. Venue can be waived or it can be conferred by consent.

- **State court-** Test considers location of P/D/ and the forum where c.o.a arose
- **Federal Court-** test considers: (A) Where the D resides; (B) where the cause of action arose; or (C) where a substantial part of the events giving rise to the cause of acion occurred or where the property that is the subject of the action is located.
- **28 U.S.C s 1391(B)** Provides that venue is proper:
- **1.** In any district where a D resides if all the D's reside in the same state; or
- **2.** In any district where a substantial part of the acts or omissions giving rise to the cause of action occurred; or
- **3.** In any district where any D is subject to personal jurisdiction, if there is no other district in which the action might be brought

<u>Federal District Courts</u> Have original jurisdiction over state-law-based suits involving citizens of difference states when the amount in controversy exceeds 75k

<u>Domicile:</u> A persons domicile is determined by: 1. Residence in that state; and 2. An intent to remain in that state.

- Determination turns on an inquiry into the individuals intent
- Courts look at a variety of factors, none of which is dispositive on its own in an attempt to determine the individuals true, fixed, permanent home and the place to which he/she intends to return when absent
- **Factors:** location of property, voting behavior, location of bank accounts, memberships/personal associations/ automobile registration/ place of employment

<u>Special Appearance-</u> State won't obtain PJ over person who appears for the sole purpose of objecting to the forum exercise of jurisdiction over him/her.

<u>Affidavit-</u> A statement under oath, must be based on personal knowledge, show the affiant is competent to testify, set forth admissible facts and attach sworn of certified copies of documents referred to.

<u>4(K)</u> A federal court may exercise personal jurisdiction to the same extent as a state court of general jurisdiction in the state where the district court sits

<u>Tort-</u> The rights and liabilities of the parties with respect to an issue in tort are determined by the local law of the state which, with respect to that issue has the most significant relationship to the occurrence and the parties.

- **Analysis-** 1. Place where the injury occurred
- **2.** The place where the conduct causing the injury occurred;

- **3**. Place of incorporation/ place of business of the parties; and
- **4**. Place where the relationship, if any, between the parties is centered.

<u>Diversity (28 U.S.C. S 1332)</u>- To satisfy diversity the amount in controversy in the action must exceed $75,000 and the parties must be diverse.

- **Citizenship**- For purposes of determining citizenship an individual is a citizen of the state in which he/she is domiciled.
- **Legal Representative/ Executor**- Shall be deemed to be a citizen only of the same state as the decedent.

<u>Service by Email FRCP 4 (Corporation outside of US)</u>- In a proper case, Federal court has the power to permit a P to serve a corporate D by email.

- Rule 4 authorizes service of process upon a corporation outside of the US in any manner prescribed by Rule 4(F) except personal delivery
- Subdivision F gives the District Court broad authority to direct service by any means not prohibited by international agreement, including means authorized by foreign law/ general international practice.

<u>Rule 11 Safe Harbor</u>- Allows attorney to cure alleged violation within 21 days of filing the pleading before the opposing party may seek the imposition of sanctions under the rule.

- Does not apply if the court on its own raises rule 11 violations.

<u>FRCP 8 Pleadings</u>- A pleading that states a claim for relief must contain:

1. A short and plain statement of the grounds for the courts jurisdiction, unless the court already had jurisdiction and the claim needs no new jurisdictional support;
2. A short and plain statement of the claim showing that the pleaded is entitled to relief; and
3. A demand for the relief sought, which may include relief in the alternative or different types of relief.

<u>FRCP 8(B) Defenses/Admissions and Denials</u>:

1. In responding to a pleading, a party must:
   A. State in short and plain terms its defenses to each claim asserted against it; and
   B. Admit or deny the allegations asserted against it by the opposing party.
- Denial- Must fairly respond to the substance of the allegation
- General denial- A party who intends in Good Faith to deny all allegations of the pleading (including jurisdiction) may do so by general denial.
- A party who does not intend to deny all allegations must specifically designate allegations or generally deny all allegations except for the specifics admitted

Discovery

<u>26(B)(1)</u>- A party may obtain discovery regarding any matter that is not privileged and that is relevant to a claim or defense in the action.

- **Relevant information-** is discoverable, even if it would be inadmissible at the trial, so long as it appears to be reasonably calculated to lead to the discovery of relevant information.

26(A) Initial Disclosures- A party must within 14 days of the 26(F) conference must provide:

1. The name and if known, the address and telephone number of each individual likely to have discoverable information
2. A copy of all documents, electronically stored information and tangible things that the disclosing party has it its possession, custody or control and may use to support its claims or defenses
3. A computation of damages; and
4. Information of insurance coverage which may satisfy all or part of a judgment.
   Experts: Parties are required to disclose experts who may be used at trial. Includes their qualifications, compensation

Personnel Records: Are discoverable despite claims that they should be protected for policy reasons. If discovery is resisted, court must balance interest of party seeking discovery vs. party withholding.

- Court may limit access by restricting access to those portions deemed clearly relevant to the action
- Alternatively, a court might order an in camera review of the records to determine whether they contain anything particularly sensitive/private.

Accident/Investigative Reports: Only protected when are prepared in response to a threat of immediate litigation.

Rule 56- Summary Judgment- Purpose is to determine whether a trial is necessary. Asks whether there are disputed facts for jury to determine.

- **Standard:** In viewing the evidence in the light most favorable to the non-moving party, the moving party must show that there are no material facts in dispute that rise to a triable level so the moving party is entitled to judgment as a matter of law.
- **Timing:** May do so at commencement of the action—up to 30 days after close of all discovery
- **All evidence considered (unlike 12(B)**
- **Procedure-** Movant burden to show no genuine disputes as to a material fact via pleadings, deposition transcripts, etc. Then if he meets burden, shifts to respondent to show there is a genuine issue for trial.

Spoilation: In general, spoliation of evidence (destruction or alteration) is improper if the party who destroyed it has notice that the evidence is relevant to litigation or should have known that it would be relevant to future litigation.

- It is improper for a party to destroy ESI relevant to pending litigation, even if destruction occurs before there is any request/order seeking it

- Duty to preserve evidence applies to a party who anticipates litigation, even if litigation has not yet been commenced
- **ESI-** States that in the absence of exceptional circumstances, parties should not be sanctioned for the loss of ESI when the loss occurs pursuant to a routine, good-faith-operation of an ESI system. However, when a party anticipates litigation, it must suspend its routine document renention/destruction policy and put in place a litigation hold to ensure preservation of the relevant documents.

Sanctions: in determining appropriate sanctions for spoliation, courts consider both the level of culpability of the spoilating party and the degree of prejudice that the loss of evidence has caused the other party.

- Federal courts have inherent power to control the litigation and can sanction misbehavior, even where there has been no specific violations of FRCP
- **Range-** the range of available sanctions is broad. It can include such sanctions as a payment of expenses incurred by the other party as a result of the destruction of the evidence, an instruction to the jury authorizing it to draw an adverse inference from the destruction of the evidence, a shifting of a burden of proof on the relevant issue or even judgment against the responsible party

49(A) Special Verdict- Consists of the jury's answers to specific factual questions on which it is instructed to make findings. The judge then applies the law to those findings and enters the appropriate judgment

49(B) General Verdict- Simply the verdict granting victory to one side or another.

- **General verdict w/ interrogatories-** When judge requires a general verdict be supporting by the juries specific findings of fact
- **After both court then enters judgment under rule 58**

Family Law

UCCJEA- Four bases upon which a court may assert jurisdiction to make an initial child custody determination:

1) The state is the home state of the child at the time of the commencement of the proceeding
2) The child and at least one contestant have a significant connection with the state;
3) The child is physically present in the state and has been abandoned or subject to abuse; or
4) No other state appears to have jurisdiction under the Act, or the state with jurisdiction has declined to exercise it and it is in the best interests of the child for the court to assert jurisdiction.

Home State- If the state is the home of the child on the date of the commencement of the proceedings or was the home state of the child within 6 months before the proceeding and the parent is absent from the state, but a parent or person acting as a parent continues to live in this state and no other states courts would have jurisdiction or other courts having jurisdiction have declined to exercise it.

Under UCCJEA-If no home state- Court may exercise jurisdiction over a child custody determination if:

A. The child and at least one parent have a significant with the state other than mere physical presence; and
B. Substantial evidence is available in the state concerning the child's care, protection, training and personal relationships

Premarital Agreement- Although courts were once hostile to premarital agreements, today all states permit spouses to contract prematurely with respect to rights and obligations in property.

- In all states, the enforcement of such agreement turns on 3 factors: 1. Voluntariness, 2. Unconscionability and 3. Disclosure. *How courts apply these factors varies from one state to the next.*
- **Uniform Premarital Agreement Act (UPAA) Adopted in 27 Jurisdictions** the party against whom enforcement is sought must prove: 1. Involuntariness; or 2. That the agreement was unreasonable when it was executed and that he/she did not receive or waive a full and reasonable disclosure and not have or could not have reasonably had an adequate knowledge of the others assets and obligations

Separation Agreement: All states authorize the invalidation of SA or a specific portion of an agreement based on a finding of fraud or unconscionability. Unconscionability doctrine will not serve to relieve a spouse whose complaint is that she believes has made a bad bargain. (equitable, not equal)

- Factors: asset non-disclosure/ access to independent counsel.

Premarital Agreement- Governs property distribution at divorce. In determining whether it is enforceable, courts consider:

1. Whether the agreement voluntarily made;
2. Whether the agreement is substantively fair; and
3. Whether full disclosure of assets/obligations was made.

- **Factors for voluntariness:** Based on presentation of agreement very close to wedding date. Analysis includes: 1. The difficulty of conferring with independent counsel; 2. Financial losses/embarrassment arising from cancellation of the wedding; and. Other reasons for proceeding with the marriage (e.x. pre-existing pregnancy). Some states consider unconscionability at time of signing and others determine at time of divorce.

- **UPAA** (Adopted in 25 states)—Party against whom enforcement is sought must prove:
1. Involuntariness; and

2. That the agreement was unconscionable when it was executed and that he/she didn't receive or waive "fair and reasonable" disclosure and "did not have or reasonable could not have had, an adequate knowledge" of the other's assets and obligations.

- **Jurisdiction-** Some states apply the law of the state in which a premarital contract was executed in determining its enforceability. Interest of state in assuring that contracts executed and marriage consummated within its borders comply with its policies.

- **Child Support/ Custody Provisions-** Traditional rule is that premarital agreement cannot bind a court deciding child support/custody. Although UPAA doesn't explicitly bar "custody provisions which are injurious to the child's best interests".

UIFSA Child Support

Order Modification- Interstate enforcement and modification of child support is governed by the uniform interstate family support act, which has been adopted in all states

Jurisdiction Under UIFSA- The state that originally issued a child support order has continuing, exclusive jurisdiction to modify the order if that state remains the residence of the oblige, obligor or the child and all parties do not consent to jurisdiction in another forum.

- Federal law requires that states, as a condition to receive federal child support funding to adopt rules that absolutely forbid the **retroactive** modification of child support obligations
- **Prospective** modification of child support order is typically available only when the petitioner can show a substantial change in circumstances. A significant decrease in income is typically a substantial change. However, when a parent seeks to modify b/c a voluntary reduction in income, a court will not modify the obligation based solely on that.

Common Law Marriage: 'Under accepted conflict of law principles, a marriage valid under the law of the place in which it was contracted is valid elsewhere unless it violates a strong public policy of the state which has the most significant relationship with the spouses and the marriage". A common law marriage, once established, is the equivalent of a ceremonial marriage.

- To Establish a CL marriage, the proponent must show:
- 1. Capacity to enter a marital contract
- 2. A present agreement (not future) that 2 parties are married;
- 3. Cohabitation; and
- 4. Holding out a marital relationship to the community

<u>Ex-parte Divorce</u>-Courts jurisdiction extends only to the marriage itself. Unless the court has personal jurisdiction over the defendant spouse, it may not issue a binding order affecting personal rights such as property division.

- **Personal Jurisdiction**- Unless a defendant is personally served within the forum state, a court does not have personal jurisdiction over a defendant who lacks minimum contacts with the state.

<u>Marital Property</u>- An asset is marital property if it was acquired during the marriage by any means other than gift, descent or devise. An asset that is initially separate property may be transformed into marital property if marital funds or significant effort by the owner-spouse during the marriage enhances its value.

- *In all states, marital property is divided at divorce without regard to how that property is legally titled*

<u>Property Division Award</u>- Divides assets of the marriage based on the equities at the time of divorce. Although a support order award may be modified after a divorce decree has entered, a property division award, whether resulting from a judicial decision or a divorce settlement agreement may not be modified after a division decree has entered.

- Property division award- Divides assets accrued during the marriage based on the equities at the time of divorce
- Property division thus reflects an evaluation of the past (while a support determination reflects an evaluation of the future) and because the past can be ascertained, property division award is not subject to post-divorce modification
- Because the past can be ascertained, courts are not empowered to reconsider that evaluation courts are not empowered to reconsider that evaluation and modify a property division award once it has been embodied in a final judgment of divorce.

Valid marriage –

1. Age – must be 18 or get parent permission
2. Capacity –
3. <u>Cannot already be married- Bigamy</u>.

<u>Alimony Factors</u>

1. Length of marriage
2. Age of parties
3. Employability
4. Contribution to family unit
5. Future acquisition of assets
6. Fault.

7. Longer the marriage -→ goes in pot.

Unwed Father- When an unwed father demonstrates a full commitment to the responsibilities of parenthood by coming forward to participate in the rearing of his child, his interest in personal contact with the child acquires substantial protection under the 14th amendments due process clause. – entitled to a hearing to demonstrate his parental unfitness prior to his rights being terminated.

Lying about paternity- If wife fails to alter husband to possibility he isn't father, could be a misrepresentation that would support a finding of fraud. As such, the conduct may serve as a basis to invalidate a child support agreement

Troxel v. Granville- Unconstitutional where a statute authorized court to grant visitation whenever it found that visitation would serve the childs best interests.

- Why? → The statute provided inadequate protection for a parents constitutionally protected liberty interest in the care, custody and control of her child. (Statute required court to give no special weight to parental determination of what the childs best interests were)

Two Married Spouses and One wants to require the other do something: American courts have consistently treated the disputes of intact families as private matter that should be resolved at home. (Even when the spouse comes to court wishes to enforce a premarital agreement, courts have refused to intervene in the disputes of couples who are living together)

- Although courts will not intervene in disputes between parents in an intact household, the state, pursuant to its jurisdiction over child abuse and neglect may obtain an order overruling a parental decision and ordering appropriate services including medical care when the parent-child-rearing decisions endanger the child
- The fact that parental rights are constitutionally protected does not alter the result, even when the parental decision is religious motivated. '*The power of a parent, even when linked to a Free Exercise Claim may be subject to limitation if it appears that parental decisions will jeopardize the health/safety of the child.*
- Although courts may not inquire into parents general religious beliefs, it may inquire into religious practices if such practices may adversely affect the physical/mental health or safety of the child.

- With respect to parental rights, the Establishment clause forbids a court to favor one religion. Although the court cannot evaluate the religion, it can instead evaluate the parents ability to provide for the physical and mental needs of the child.
- A child custody determination is decided on the basis of the Best Interests of the Child. Under which the court is free to consider a wide range of factors.

Family Privacy Doctrine- A court may not order one parent to follow the child-rearing preferences of the other parents when the parents live together with the child in an intact family.

Common Law Jurisdiction(non-community property): If mother in father live in a CL jurisdiction in an intact household, father will have no management powers with respect to mothers earnings.

- Under Common Law, when a woman married, her identity was swallowed up by her husbands. As a result, married woman couldn't own property. → Mid 19th Century, Legislatures began to enact 'Married Woman's Property Acts' that restored to married woman the right to acquire, own and transfer property.
- Because each spouse has the full management rights with respect to his/her earnings, a court will not overrule the spending decisions of a spouse based on his/her partners conclusion that those decisions are ill advised
- Marriage, however, does create support obligations and based on SCOTUS decision in Orr v. Orr- those obligations have been gender neutral- based on the mutual support obligation a creditor who has furnished necessities to a H/W may sue the spouse of the purchaser and recover on the debt. However necessaries is only available to a creditors who has already provided goods/services, such creditor has no power to obtain an order altering a spouses future spending.

Veto Unmarried fathers right to veto adoption:

A. Applies when a non-resident father provided minimal support and did nothing to establish paternity (legally) until after an adoption petition filed; and
B. An adoption entered without notice to an unmarried father when the state provided him with an opportunity to obtain notice through registration with a 'Putative Father Registry'

Wills

<u>Exoneration-</u> Arises when a testator dies and his will devises property subject to a mortgage debt for which the testator was personally liable. Directs the mortgage be paid from assets in the residuary clause.

Agency/ Partnership

<u>Agency-</u> Is a consensual legal relationship where one party, the principal, grants another party, the agent, to act on the principals behalf to deal with third parties.

- **Formation:** Doesn't require all formalities of contract law.
- **By Agreement:** Reqs: 1. Assent of both parties- i.e. an informal agreement between a principal with capacity and the agent; 2. Benefit- the agent must work for the principals benefit; and 3. Right to control the agent—by having the power to supervise the manner of the agents performance.

    Estoppel(aka apparent authority)- Requires a 3rd parties reliance on principals actions. Apparent authority is created by a persons manifestations that another has authority to act with legal consequences for the person who makes the manifestations. When a 3rd party reasonably believes the actor to be authorized and the belief is traceable to the manifestation.

    Requires:1. Principal cloaks agent with appearance of authority (ask *What did the principal do to create a reasonable belief in the mind of the 3rd party that Agent had authority; and 2.* Reliance by 3rd party on that appearance

- **Termination of Apparent Authority:** Termination of actual authority by itself doesn't terminate. Apparent authority ends when it is no longer for the 3rd party with whom the agent deals to continue to believe that agent acts with actual authority

    By Ratification- When authority is conferred by the principal after agent has already entered into the contract. In these cases, the agent purports to act on behalf of the principal despite the fact the agent doesn't have the authority to do so, but the principal subsequently ratifies the transaction.

    ------<u>Elements:</u> 1. Principal must have knowledge of all the material facts; 2. Must accept the contracts benefits; MUST ACCEPT ALL BENEFITS and MUST RATIFY THE K as it is; and 3. Principal has capacity (i..e mentally competent and of legal age)

    Capacity: *Principal-* Individual needs capacity, no minors/incompetents

    Agent- Generally any person can be an agent, includes minors

Equal Dignity Rule- Generally, no writing is required for agency agreement. **EXCEPT** if the contract is one within the Statute of Frauds (land) then written authorization is required for someone else to legally enter into the contract on your behalf.

Actual authority: When agent and principal have agreed either expressly or impliedly that the agent will act on behalf of the principal in a certain capacity.

Terminates- Lapse of time/ Occurrence of stated event/ Change in circumstances/ Agent's breach of fiduciary duty/ Unilateral termination by either party/ Operation of law (i.e. death/incapacity of principal/agent)

- Actual (express) authority- When principal expressly authorizes the agent with written or spoken words to enter into the K.
- Actual (implied) authority: Authorization inferred from conduct or circumstances. (i.e. the authority that the agent reasonably believes she possesses as a result of the principals actions)
- Recovable: Actual authority is revocable by either party at anytime or by death/incapacity of the principal. EXCEPT: Durable power of attorney is irrevocable upon death.

Irrevocable Agencies: (A) Agency Coupled with an interest- If agent herself has an interest in the SM of the agency then not revocable before expiration of the interest unless there is some agreement to the contrary (EX: I borrow 20k from you to buy a car you want me to sell for you)

(B) Power given as security

Duties of Agent: Fiduciary duty to exercise reasonable care/ obey reasonable instructions/ duty of loyalty

- **Principals Remedies:** 1. May recover loss caused by breach; and 2. May disgorge profits made my agent (secret profits)

Duties of principal: To provide reasonable compensation to agent (if agreement silent) to indemnify agent for expenses

- **Agents Remedies:** Contractual remedies for breach/ possessory lien from any $ due principal

Liability for Tort (respondeat Superior) Principal will be liable for torts committed by agent if: 1. Principal-agent relationship and 2. Tort occurred within the scope of employment

- 3 Part test for determining if in scope of employment- 1. If the task was within the scope of the job description then within scope of agency; 2. Tort occurred on the job; and 3. Conduct intended for the Principal's benefit

- **Intentional Torts:** Liability 1. Specifically authorized by principal; 2. Part of the Nature of employment or 3. Motivated by a desire to serve the principal.

Frolic- A new and independent journey which is outside the scope of agency

Detour- A mere departure from an assigned task and is still within the scope of agency.

Independent Contracts: Without the right to control, there is no vicarious liability for independent contractor torts unless:

1) Ultra-hazardous activities- ind contractor commits tort while engage in these
2) Estoppel- Principal holds out an independent contractor with the appearance of agency, he will be precluded from denying agency to idk k
3) Non-delegable duties
4) Principal knowingly selected incompetent contractor

Negligent Hiring- A principal can be found liable for the negligent hiring of an agent (i.e failure to do a background check) or negligent retention after becoming aware the agents unfitness.

Contract Liability- A principal is liable for contracts entered into by her agent if the principal authorized the agent to enter into the K.

Authorization for Ks

1. Actual Express Authority- via words to enter into a k
2. Actual Implied Authority- Authorization inferred from conduct or circumstances
3. Apparent Authority- If there is an appearance of authority to 3rd party
4. Ratification- Authority conferred by Principal after A has already entered into K

- **Agents Contract Authority –**
  If unauthorized- A liable | Authorized- Generally, agent is not liable for contracts entered into o/b/o a principal

- <u>Undisclosed/Partially Disclosed Principal:</u> An authorized agent may be liable even on an authorized contract when the principal is undisclosed or partially disclosed at the election of the 3rd party. 3rd party may sue either the agent or the principal after disclosure.

-

2nd Restatement	3rd Restatement
Undisclosed Principal cannot ratify at K	Principal will be liable when he/she does ratify the K (**Under 2nd/3rd Agent will be liable as a party to the K**)
	No apparent authority in case of undisclosed principal b/c no manifestations from principal to 3rd party

General Partnership

General Partnership- An association of two or more persons who carry on as co-owners of a business for profit. Governed by the RUPA, however, partners are free to govern their relationship by different rules but RUPA will govern issue not addressed in their agreement.

> ** Persons can be individual, corporation, partnership, trust or other entity

Common Property ownership- Not enough to create a partnership. But if you do something in addition to owning common property then can create.

Partners- Jointly and Severally liable for the obligations of the partnership unless otherwise agreed or provided by law.

- A partnership created to engage in illegal activity is void
- **Notice**: A partner has notice of a fact if the partner: 1. Knows of it; 2. Has received a notification of it; or 3. Has reason to know it exists from all the facts known to the person at the time in question

Binding Partnership—Under RUPA the act of any partner for apparently carrying on the ordinary course of the partnership business or the business of the kind carried out by the partnership binds the partnership.

- Except: When the partner had no authority to act for the partnership in the matter; and 3rd party knew or had received notification that the partner lacked authority
  --→ Knowledge: A person knows a fact if the person has actual knowledge of it/ Or has received notification which is either i. duly delivered at the persons place of business or ii. Comes to the person's attention

Profit/Losses- Without an agreement to the contrary, partners share these equally.

Additional Rights: Right to indemnification for expenses incurred on behalf of the partnership in the ordinary course of business, right to equal control, unanimous consent required for a person to become a new member, each partner has equal rights in the management and conduct of the business. Rights to inspect and copy the partnership books, duty to account true and full information about all things affecting the partnership.

Personal Liability- Each partner is personally liable for the debts & obligation of the partnership. If one partner pays more than a fair share he/she is entitled to compensation from the other members.

- **Torts-** Partners are personally liable for torts committed by fellow partners in the scope of usual partnership business
- **Contracts-** Partners are personally liable for the authorized contracts enter into by partners with partnership authority.

- **Crimes-** No partner will be criminally liable for the crimes committed by other partners within the scope of the partnership, unless he/she was a principal or accessory to the crime.

Duties of Partners (FIDUCIARY)

- Duty of care- No reckless, negligent or unlawful conduct

Duty of loyalty: Requires: No secret profits at Partnership's expense = Account for all profits & benefits derived in connection with the Partnership Business; No self dealing (i..e refrain from Dealing with partnership as an adverse interest) and 3. No usurping Partnership opportunities (i.e. cant compete with partnership)

- **Partnership Remedies for Breach-** Action for accounting/ Can recover losses caused by breach. Disgorge profits made by breaching partner

Dissociation: A change in the relation of the partners caused by any partner cerasing to be associated in the carrying on" partnership caused by express will of any partner no longer being associated with the partnership.

- A partner has the power to dissociate at anytime, rightfully or wrongfully by express words

- **Wrongful Dissociation:** Would be wrongful if partnership agreement required giving 6 months notice. A wrongfully dissociating partner could not participate in the winding up of the business. If one partner causes this in contravention to the terms of the partnership agreements, other partners have a right to damages for the breach of the partnership agreement.

- Remaining partners can waive the right to have the partnership terminated and the business wound up. If the remaining partners did this, the would have the chance to purchase the wrongfully dissociating partners interest for a buyout price determined in accordance w/ s. 701(B)

- **UPA** "A rightful or wrongful withdrawal results in the dissolution of the partnership. However, the partners who have not caused the dissolution wrongfully, if they desire to continue the business in the same name may do so, a partner who caused the wrongful dissolution is not granted the same right"

Dissolution: Requires a partnership business to be wound up. Dissolution only begins the process of ending a partnership. Partnership continues after dissolution only for the purpose of winding up its business and partnership is terminated when the winding up of its business is complete.

- **Cause(s):** Partnership at will- when partnership has notice of that partners express will to withdraw/ Occurrence of a stated event/ Court order upon a partners application

<u>Winding up General Partnership:</u> The period between dissolution and the termination in which the remaining partners liquidate partnerships assets and satisfy the partnerships debts and obligations.

- **Priority of Distribution:** 1. Creditors; 2. Partners accounts
- **Partnership Liability during winding up:** A partnership is bound by partners act after dissolution if the act was appropriate to the winding up of the partnership. If the partnership is bound, then each partner is liable for his proportionate share of the liability. (All partners are jointly and severally liable for all obligations of the partnership)

<u>Election:</u> A general partnership can make an election and become a LLP if: the parties approve the conversion by a vote equivalent to that necessary to amend the partnership agreement. Then the partnership files a statement of qualification, containing its principal office address and election to be an LLP.

- **Claim arises before LLP status obtained-** Then partners remain personally liable on that claim
- **LLP** partners may still be liable if any one of the partners is negligent/acts wrongful.

<u>Incoming Partner-</u> While general rule is that partners of a GP are J&S liable for all obligations of the partnership, there is a special rule for partners who are admitted during the duration of the partnership.

- Under UPA- a person admitted to an existing partnership is not personally liable for any partnership obligations incurred before the persons admission

<u>Additional Liabilities of Partners:</u> Partners are liable for misrepresentations made by the other partners provided that they are acting in the ordinary course of partnership business.

- If no statement that limits one of the partners purported authority- Then will be an agent of the partnership for the purpose of its business
- Intentional misrepresentations in the ordinary course of business- wrongful act creates a partnership obligation for which each are J&S liable.

Limited Partnership

<u>Limited Partnership:</u> A limited partnership is composed of one or more general partners and one or more limited partners. Governed by RULPA.

- **General Partner:** Fully liable in individual capacity for debts/obligations in both tort and contract
- <u>Rights:</u> Rights to manage the business, right to vote on any matter pertaining to partnership
- **Limited Partner:** Not liable

- **Rights:** No right to manage, right to vote on any matter, right to bring derivative action (if GP refuse to do so) right to obtain partnership info, includes: 1. Inspect/copy books and records; 2. Tax records; 3. Obtain from GP info regarding the financial info
- Limited Partner will be personally liable if: 1. He is also a General partner; 2. He participates in the control of the business; or 3. Liable to creditors who extend credit to LP who acted w/o knowledge that limited partner not a general partner

Structure: Must file a Certification of Limited Partnership with the Secretary of State Office

- Must contain 'Limited Partnership' without abbreviation on the certificate
- General partner must sign the initial certificate of limited partnership filed → if filed without signature of GP = prevents formation of LP
- If it has the name of the limited partner then Must have the name of the general partner
- Must have the name & address of the Agent for Service of Process
- Name and business address of Each General partner and
- Latest Date upon which the LP is to dissolve

Records: LP must continuously maintain in the state of organization, an office (which may but need not be its place of business) at which it keeps: the certificate of organization, LP agreement, Partnership tax returns/financial statements for 3 most recent years.

Profits: If the partnership agreement is silent then profits and losses are allocated on the basis of the contributions made by each partner

Limited Liability Partnership (LLP)

LLP- No partner is personally liable for obligations of the partnership. Each will be personally liable for his/her own torts.

Requires: Filing a statement of qualification, statement electing to be an LLP, Filing annual report at Secretary of states office, Current office of CEO office

Failure to file annual report: Basis for Secretary of State to administratively revoke its statement of qualification.

Members: Courts hold that members of an LLC, like partners in a GP are in a fiduciary relationship. Direct competition is usually a violation of the duty of loyalty.

Liability: General rule that LLC members not personally liable for debts of the firm doesn't apply when: 1. The proper procedures for dissolution and winding up haven't been followed; and 2. A court decides to "pierce the LLC veil"

- **Piercing the veil:** Common-law equitable doctrine that prevents members from hiding behind the veil of limited liability in situations where they have improperly used the LLC form. Analysis focuses on whether the members have treated the LLC as a separate entity or whether it has become the alter ego of its members. If the latter is true, members will not enjoy immunity from individual liability for LLC's acts that cause damage to third parties. Each member for whom the veil is pierced becomes subject to joint & several liability to the creditor bringing the claim.

- **Factors for piercing:** Siphoning corporate funds, use of business funds for personal use, intermingling of personal/business funds

Dissolution: (Statement of Cancellation Required)LLP dissolved and its affairs shall be wound up upon the occurrence of either: time stated in Certificate of Limited Partnership, Upon the happening of events stated in the agreement, by written consent of all partners, withdrawal of Genreal partner.

- LLC must provide notice of dissolution as part of its winding up process to creditors so that they can make claims against the dissolving entity. → Notice must outline the steps necessary for enforcing their claims.
- If procedures aren't followed and the LLC's assets have been liquidated/distributed to its members, then creditors claim against the LLC may be enforced against each of the LLC members to the extent of the members proportionate share of the claim or to the extent of LLC assets distributed, whichever is less. However, a member's total liability for creditor claims may not exceed the total value of assets distributed to the member in dissolution
- **Distribution of Assets:** 1. To the creditors (included partner who are ordinary creditors of LP) 2. To partners and former partners in satisfaction of liability for interim distributions and distributions due on withdrawal; 3. To partners for return of contribution; 4. Profits and Property to partners.

LLC Operating Agreement- Members of an LLC can agree to restrict or limit the duty of loyalty, provided the opt-out is specified in the operating agreement. As long as it isn't "manifestly unreasonable" the operating agreement may also identify specific types or categories of activities that do not violate the duty of loyalty.

Corporations

MBCA – Corporate existence begins when the articles of incorporation are filed.

Before Filing: "All persons purporting to act as or on behalf of a corporation, knowing there was no incorporation are jointly and severally liable for all liabilities created while so acting"

- De-facto incorporation doctrine: A shareholder not liable for the obligations of a defectively incorporated corporation when there was a "bona fide attempt to organize and colorable or apparent compliance with the requirements of the law"
- Personally liable: If articles of incorporation not filed and person who purports to act on behalf of a corporation not yet formed possesses actual knowledge that the corporations charter has not been issued.

Articles of Incorporation: May include a provision that shields directors from liability for money damages for the failure to exercise adequate care in the performance of their duties as directors.

- **Permitted provisions:** Those that protect directors from liability for breaches of the duty of care
- **Prohibited provisions:** Those that protect directors from breach of duty of loyalty, acts/omissions not done in good faith or any transaction in which director receives an improper personal benefit

<u>Stock Splits:</u> Are events that increase the number of shares outstanding and reduce the par/stated value per share. EX: 2-for-1 stock split- a shareholder owning 1,000 shares out of 100,000 would now own 2,000 shares out of 200,000

<u>Stock Dividends:</u> The issuance of additional shares of stock to existing shareholders on a proportional basis. EX: A shareholder who owns 100 shares of stock will own 125 after a 25% stock dividend.

<u>Internal Affairs of Corporation:</u> Such as the conduct of shareholder meetings and election of directors are subject to the corporate law of the state of incorporation.

- Procedures for nominating directors are found in bylaws
- "Business and Affairs"- of the corporation are managed by the board. Although shareholders are limited generally to adopting precatory resolutions that recommend or encourage board action, the limitation doesn't apply when the shareholders have specific authority to take action on their own- such as amending bylaws.

<u>Amending Bylaws:</u> Under MBCA, shareholders have power to amend the bylaws. The board shares this power with the shareholders, unless: (1) The corporations articles reserve that power exclusively to the shareholders; or (2) The shareholders, in amending, repealing or adopting a bylaw expressly provide that the board may not amend, repeal or reinstate that bylaw.

- A shareholder bylaw can generally limit the power of the board to later amend or repeal it

<u>Derivative Suit:</u> One brought in the right of a domestic corporation. If it claims breach of fiduciary duties to the corporation. MBCA requires shareholders make a written demand on the board of directors and 90 days expire before initiating suit.

- Claim is brought to vindicate corporate rights. Demand permits the board to investigate the situation identified by the shareholder and take suitable action.

<u>Direct Suit-</u> Vindicates shareholders own rights in a suit in his/her individual capacity to enforce an individual right of a shareholder. No demand required.

- EX: Suit to compel payment of a dividend. (Would be shareholders right to share in the net profits of the corporation)

<u>Business Judgment Rule:</u> Protects directors from liability for breach of their fiduciary duties. Is a presumption that in making business decisions, the directors act on an informed basis, in good faith, and in the honest belief that the action being taken is in the best interest of the corporation. If directors do not qualify for this protection, they will be found in breaching of their duty of care in approving a contract.

- **Becoming informed:** in performing their duty to become informed, directors are generally entitled to rely upon information, reports, opinions of the corporate officers.
- Where a director sits on both sides of a transaction, the BJR doesn't apply.
- If Director is interest in the transaction, he will be required to establish the fairness of the transaction in question in order to avoid a claim that he breached a fiduciary duty of loyalty
- **Statutory safe harbor-** where transactions are approved by disinterested directors and therefore immune from attack. <u>Requires:</u> director disclose all material facts about his/her interest in the transaction. *Material facts:* Those an ordinarily prudent person would reasonably believe to be material to a judgment about whether or not to proceed with the transaction. – Duty of loyalty claim can be rebutted by proof that the transaction "judged according to the circumstances at the time of commitment, is established to have been fair to the corporation"

<u>Shareholders Rights:</u> A shareholder has the right to inspect corporate books and records for a proper purpose. A proper purpose is a purpose reasonably related to a person's interest as a shareholder.

<u>Annual Shareholders meeting:</u> Only shareholders on the record date are entitled to vote.

- **Record date:** Determines who is entitled to vote at a particular shareholder meeting. "Namely those persons who were registered as shareholders of records on that date".
- **Selling shares after record date:** Doesn't give subsequent purchaser to vote because occurred after record date. Shareholder of record is entitled to vote the shares (absent a proxy to another)
- **Shareholder proxies:** A shareholder may vote in person or in proxy. Are generally revocable and any action inconsistent with the grant of a proxy works as a revocation of that proxy. <u>Except:</u> 'If the proxy form explicitly says irrevocable and the shareholder is coupled with an interest"
- **Counting shares:** In counting shares, each outstanding share is entitled to one vote on each matter voted on at a shareholder's meeting
- **If there is a conflict between articles of Incorporation and the Bylaws regarding how many shares must vote in favor of a proposal in order for the proposal to be approved, the articles of incorporation preempt. **ANY bylaw that conflicts with the articles of incorporation is void****

<u>Special Meetings:</u> Unless articles specify otherwise, Must be given at least 2 days prior to the date of meeting, include the time/location/date of meeting. Doesn't need to include purpose.

- A director who does not receive notice of a special meeting of the board at least 2 days prior doesn't receive proper notice. However, if he attends the meeting despite not receiving proper notice he waives such notice <u>unless</u> the director objects to the holding of the meeting and thereafter doesn't vote at such meeting.

- **Action taken at special meeting:** require a quorum to be present at the meeting for action to be proper. Unless the articles of incorporation or the bylaws provide otherwise, when a corporation has a fixed number of directors, a quorum consists of a majority of that fixed number.

- **Participation via telephone-** Although directors can generally participate at special meetings over the phone, such participation is valid only if all directors participating may simultaneously hear each other during the meeting.

Dissolving: A proposal to dissolve the corporation adopted by board of directors must be submitted to a shareholder vote.

Close Corporations

- Fiduciary duties owed by majority shareholders.
- Duty to disclose any information that knows is material/ necessary for a reasonable shareholder to consider in deciding how to vote on a transaction
- Ask: 1. Was non-disclosure by majority shareholder material? 2. Did the non-disclosure cause any loss to the minority shareholders?
- **Majority Shareholder purchasing Majority interest-** has a duty of fair dealing. Burden would be on majority shareholder to demonstrate that the process it employed was fair and that the price it selected was fair.

LLC

Member managed- Members do not have the right to maintain a direct action against the manager when the alleged misconduct caused harm only to the LLC. (i.e. failing to manage the business properly)

Derivative action- can be maintained for mismanagement of an LLC. In order to maintain, they must make a demand that the manager bring the action and allege in their complaint the efforts the made to secure initiation of the action by the manager or the reasons for not making the demand effort.

Business Judgment Rule- Protects LLC managers from liability for business decisions made in good faith. Court will not second guess managers decision, even it was a bad one, if the manager acted on an informed basis, in good faith and in the honest belief that the action taken was in the best interests of the company"

Veil Piercing- Ordinarily, members of an LLC are not liable for the debts, obligations or liabilities of LLC solely by reason of being/acting as a member. Two theories of veil piercing:

- 1. Mere instrumentality- Must show- a) The members dominated the entity in such a way that the LLC had no will of its own; b) The members used that domination to commit a fraud or wrong; and c) The control and wrongful action proximately caused the injury complained of

- 2. Unity of interest and ownership- Must demonstrate that there was such a unity of interest and ownership between the entity and members that, in fact, LLC did not have an existence independent of the members and that failure to pierce through the members would be unjust/inequitable
- Failure of an LLC to observe the usual company formalities, is not a ground for imposing personal liability on the members or its managers (ULLCA)

Property

Life tenant- A lifetime ownership of land measured in terms of lifetime, not years. Upon expiration of a life estate, interest in the property reverts to the grantor unless assigned to a third party. Must pay taxes on the land to the extent of the income/profits of the land. If none, to the extent of the reasonable rental value. If land is vacant/unproductive- no obligation to pay taxes.

- **Adverse Possession RE: Life tenancy**- A claimant permitted to tack.

EX: In this case, Olive conveyed a life estate in Blackacre to Lois. Lois then subsequently leased Blackacre to Trent for a term of 15 years at the monthly rent of $500. When Lois died intestate 11 years ago, the title to Blackacre reverted back to Olive. As such, Trent's possession of Blackacre was hostile (i.e. without Olive's permission). There is privity between Ron and Trent (i.e. landlord/tenant relationship), so Ron would be able to tack Trent's possession of Blackacre to run the required statute. Since Lois died 11 years ago and the period in which to acquire title by adverse possession in the jurisdiction is 10 years, the court should hold that title in fee simple is in Ron.

Tenant in Common- Each tenant owns an undivided one-half interest and must pay her share of the taxes, i.e. in proportion to the tenant's ownership interest.

- Right to partition: (1) Partition In Kind- Preferred when physical division of the property is possible; (2) Partition by Sale- Allowed only when a fair and equitable division of the property is impossible

Joint Tenancy- Each tenant (2 or more) owns undivided share with the right of survivorship.

- **Right of survivorship:** When one JT dies, her share automatically passes to remaining JTs
- **Severance-** Any JT can destroy right of survivorship by severing JT, if severed, becomes a Tenancy in Common

- **Conveyance:** Severs the JT as to the conveying JT's interest, but if there were more than 2 JTs, other non-conveying JT's still have JT between them w/ TIC
- **Lease by JT-** <u>CL-</u> Severs| <u>Modern Law-</u> doesn't sever JT

<u>Tenancy by Entirety-</u> Husband and wife own undivided share with the right of survivorship. Parties must be husband and wife. Immune from the claims of the separate creditors of either spouse, and creditors cannot attach to the right of survivorship.

- **Severance-** Divorce (creates TIC most states) or (JT minority)
- **Unliateral conveyance** – no SEVERANCE.

<u>Rights & Duties of Co-Tenants (JT/TIE/TIC)</u>

- Each co-tenant has the right to possess and enjoy the entire property (i.e. no ouster (wrongful exclusion) of co-tenant)
- Each tenant is entitled to share of profits from the estate (i.e. rental income from 3rd parties)
- Each co-tenant must pay her fair share of payments due on mortgages
- Each co-tenant has a right to contribution for any repairs she makes that are reasonable, necessary and communicated to the co-tenants
- Co-tenant must not commit waste and co-tenant can bring action for waste committed during the co-tenancy

<u>Recording system</u> protects bona fide purchasers and mortgagees only.

<u>Bona fide purchaser</u> is a subsequent purchaser who purchases the property for valuable consideration and without notice at the time of conveyance.

- **Notice-** Actual (i.e. literal knowledge) or constructive knowledge (i.e. inquiry or record).

<u>Wild deed</u> is defined as a recorded deed that is not in the chain of title because of a previously unrecorded deed. A wild deed does not provide record notice to later purchasers of the property, because subdqeuent bona fide purchasers cannot reasonably be expected to locate the deed while investigating the chain of title to the property.

<u>Estoppel by deed</u> is a legal doctrine under which a first party, who purports to sell real property that the first party does not actually own to a second party, must actually convey that property to the second party if the first party later acquires title to that property.

Grantor Interests

<u>Possibility of Reverter-</u> Estate automatically reverts to grantor upon occurrence of stated event. Is transferable devisable/descendible and alienable.

- Follows fee simple determinable

<u>Right of Entry-</u> Fee simply subject to condition subsequent. Doesn't happen automatically. Grantor must exercise her right of entry. Is devisable/descendible.

- Follows fee simple subject to condition subsequent

Reversion: The interest that remains after subtracting what the grantor has granted from what the grantor originally possessed. i.e.

- Follows if Grantor conveys life estate

Grantee Interests

Remainder: Future interest in a grantee upon the termination of a prior estate of known/fixed duration

- Cannot arise by operation of law.
- Created only by express grant in same instrument in which preceding possessory estate is created.
- Follows: life estate/term of years
- **Vested Remainder:** 1) Created in an ascertained person; and 2) Not subject to any condition precedent.
- **Contingent Remainder:** 1. Created in an unascertained person; or 2. Subject to a condition precedent (an act or event that must exist/occur before the remainder vests)

Executory Interest: A future interest in a grantee that divests or cuts short a defeasible fee in another grantee. In order to become possessory must divest or cut short the prior estate (shifting) or spring out of the grantor or her heirs (springing) at a future date.

- EX: "To A and her heirs, but if B returns from Canada, to B and her heirs"
- **A-** Fee Simple | **B-** Shifting executory interest

Rule Against Perpetuities- For a future interest to be valid, the interest must vest, if at all, within 21 years of some life in being at the instruments effective date. (measuring life)

- **Measuring Life:** Is a natural person who is alive when interest is created. Can be anyone, provided their identifiable and somehow connected with the vesting/failing of the interest.
- **Valid:** O grants "To A for life, remainder to A's children" – valid b/c will know when interest will vest, within 21 years after A's life. (And also when A dies)
- **Invalid:** O grants "To A for life, remainder to A's children who reach the age of 25" – Future interest in A's children is void b/c it is possible that won't vest within 21 years of A's death.

Foreclosure- is a legal proceeding to terminate a mortgagor's interest in property, instituted by the mortgagee either to gain title to the property or to force the sale in order to satisfy the unpaid debt secured by the mortgage.

- **Deficiency** is a judgment against the debtor if the sale proceeds are less than the amount of the loan, in which case the debtor is personally liable if the proceeds of the sale do not satisfy the debt and the mortgagee can bring an action against the debtor to recover the deficiency.

- **Surplus** is distributed in the following order: (1) expenses of sale, attorneys' fees and court costs, (2) accrued interest on foreclosed mortgage, (3) junior lienholders, (4) debtor

Notice Jurisdiction- Buyer will take lot free of any unrecorded deeds.

- IF- innocent purchaser for value & no notice of unrecorded document

Due on Sale Clause- Triggered when landowner conveys land without the prior consent of the bank.

- **Land installment K-** Will trigger due-on-sale clause

Implied Easement/ Easement by Necessity- Only applies if land was ever held in common ownership.

Mortgage: a consensual interest in real property, including fixtures, which secures payment or performance of an obligation.

Implied Covenant of Quiet Enjoyment- is an implied warranty that the landlord will not unreasonably interfere with the tenants use and enjoyment of the premises. This warranty applies to both residential and commercial leases and can be breached by either an actual wrongful eviction or a constructive eviction.

Constructive Eviction: There must be a substantial interference caused by the landlord (or which the landlord has notice of but fails to act), the tenant must provide notice of the substantial interference and move out within a reasonable time after LL fails to remedy the problem/ terminate all future rent payments.

Implied Warranty of Habitability: At CL, a tenants duty to pay rent was considered independent of the landlords duty to provide the premises. Caveat emptor was the rule of the day. Courts have abandoned this rule and applies a covenant of habitatbility in RESIDENTIAL leases only. Thus, if a landlord provides premises that are uninhabitable, the tenants duty to pay rent may be excused.

- **Tenant remedies:** Move out/terminate lease, reduce/withhold rent/ repair and deduct

Assignment-The transfer by the lessee of her entire interest (i.e. transfers entire remaining term of leasehold)

- **Privity of K original T-** Yes original T-LL. Thus, if assignee fails to pay rent, LL can recover against the tenant if he cannot recover against assignee.
- **Privity of K LL/Assignee-** LL cannot sue assignee on privity of K because assignee didn't make the promise to LL
- **Privity of Estate-** Not between LL/Original T. – Between LL/Assignee. Privity of estate gives LL/assignee the right to sue each other.

Sublease- Occurs when a tenant transfers her rights and obligations to a subtenant for a portion of the term of the lease. The tenant retains the interest in the remaining part of the leasehold term that was not transferred.

- **Privity of K T1-T2-** Creates new LL/T relationship between T1/T2
- **LL/SL- Landlord** has no legal relationship with SL so not personally liable to her for rent b/c no privity of estate/K. ONLY possible exception is IWOH residential

Lateral & Subjacent Support: Describes the right of a landowner to have that land physically supported in its natural state by both adjoining land and underground structures. If a neighbor's excavation or excessive extraction of underground liquid causes subsidence (i.e. caused land to cave in) the neighbor will be subject to liability in tort.

Riparian Rights- All landowners whose property is adjacent to a body of water have the right to make reasonable use of it. Therefore, a riparian owner will be liable to other riparian owners if her use of the water unreasonably interferes with the other riparian owners use of the water.

Easement- A grant of a non-possessory interest in land that entitles the person to use land possessed by another (servient land)

- **Affirmative easement-** Owner has a right to go on the land of another and do some act on the land
- **Existing use easement-** If use existed before the tract was split in two or more parts and the use of the servient part was necessary for the use and enjoyment of the dominant part. **Requires:** 1) Two properties were once a single tract of land and later divided; 2. Apparent & continuous use on servient land; 3. Parties intended that use continue; and 4. Reasonably necessary to use and enjoyment of dominant land
- **By Necessity-** Implied when an owner sells a portion of her easte and the result of the sale is a landlocked parcel of land. Implied only when land is divided. Implied over a portion of a divided tract that blocks access to a public road from the landlocked parcel **Requires:1)** Previous united ownership; 2)absolute necessity and 3. Necessity existed at time of severance of the property
- **By prescription:** Easement acquired by an adverse use for the requisite period. Exclusive use is not required. **Requires:** 1) Actual use; 2) Open and notorious; 3) Adverse (hostile) cannot be by owners permission; 4) Continuous use for the statutory period
- **Negative easement:** Gives holder the right to prevent servient owner from using land in someway that would otherwise be permitted (light/air/subjacent support)

Torts

Invasion of privacy- (4 types)

- **Appropriation-** Make an unauthorized use of another's name for his own benefit
- **Intrusion-** intrude upon another's solitude
- **Publicity of Private Life-** Where on publicizes truthful details about the others private life.

- **False Light-** Where one places the other before the public in a false light. Requires that the defendant place the plaintiff before the public in a false light that would be highly offensive to a reasonable person.

Trespass: Is the invasion of land by tangible physical object. Trespass occurs when the defendant intentionally enters plaintiffs land w/o permission, the defendant remains on the land without the right to be there, even if the original entry was lawful, or the defendant places a tangible object on, or refuses to remove from plaintiffs land without permission. Trespass is the interference with the interests of exclusive possession in land (i.e. right to exclude)

Private Nuisance: A substantial and unreasonable interference with plaintiffs use and enjoyment of her land.

Trespasser- No duty of care owed to undiscovered trespassers because undiscovered trespassers are unforeseeable victims.

- **Discovered trespasser-** owner owes trespassers a duty of reasonable care.

Invitee- Persons who are invited onto the land to conduct business with the owner of the property or persons invited as a member of the public for purposes for which land is held open to the public.

Negligent Misrepresentation- Need to have a duty owed. I.E. won't apply to a job applicant and a screening doctor because the duty would only extend between Dr./Employer who retained doctor in his professional capacity to evaluate medical records of prospective employees.

Negligent infliction of emotional distress (i.e. wrongfully say that patient has aids) to another is breached (1) when the threat of physical impact leads to emotional distress or (2) there is a special relationship between plaintiff and defendant that is breached and directly causes severe emotional distress. The emotional distress must cause subsequent physical consequences (e.g. a heart attack)

Intentional Infliction of Emotional Distress requires (1) intentional or reckless infliction, (2) of severe emotional or mental distress, (3) by extreme and outrageous conduct, (4) actual damages and (5) causation

Duty of Care- a legal duty requiring the defendant to act according to a certain standard to protect a plaintiff against an unreasonable risk of injury. A duty of care is owed to all foreseeable plaintiffs and the extent of this duty is determined by the applicable standard of care. The basic standard of care is that of a reasonable person of ordinary prudence in the defendant's position

Actual Cause- Requires that but for the breach of duty by the defendant, the plaintiff would have not been injured.

Dangerous Artificial Conditions- owners and occupiers of land have duty of reasonable care to people located off the premises.

Ordinary Negligence Cases- No punitive damages available

Nuisance- Whether an invasion constitutes a nuisance depends on whether it causes a significant harm of a kind that would be suffered by a normal member of the community.

Product Defective- If it fails to include a safety device that would prevent foreseeable injuries incurred in the ordinary use.

Court- Decides questions of law | Jurors- Questions of fact

Question of law EX: (PL Case) "whether a D manufacturer should be held to the standard of a prudent manufacturer who knew of risks in 1960"

Privilege of Arrest- Defense to intentional torts

- Elements: A private citizen may arrest another without a warrant if:
- 1. A felony was actually committed; and
- The private actor has reasonable ground to believe the suspect committed the felony.

Constitutional Law

Supreme Court Jurisdiction (Art III) Supreme Court may only hear a case after there has been a final judgment. The Supreme Court has original and exclusive jurisdiction over controversies between state governments. The Supreme Court's appellate jurisdiction (i.e. writ of certiorari) over federal courts is limited to cases from the Federal Court of Appeals

Nativity Scene- The rule is that displays of religious themes are permissible so long as the religious symbols are surrounded by primarily secular symbols.

Appointments- all members of federal boards exercising executive powers must be appointed by the President or in a manner otherwise consistent with the appointments clause of Article II.

- The president appoints all ambassadors, public ministers/consuls, justice of the supreme court and all other officers of the U.S. whose appointments are not otherwise provided for with the advice/consent of the senate.
- **Congress-** May vest the appointment of inferior officers in President alone, lower Federal Courts of heads of departments. However, it is prohibited from delegating appointment power to itself or its officers.

President Powers/ Steel Seizure Tripartite Formula-

1. **Power at it's apex when-** He acts pursuant to a power given to him by Congress
2. **President power lessened when-** There is no Congressional Legislation on the Matter
3. **At their lowest-** When President Acts in the face of Congressional Legislation.

Commerce Clause- If Congress has not acted, a state or local government may regulate local aspects of interstate commerce unless the state/local laws discriminate against out of state residents or place an undue burden on interstate commerce.

- **Law will be unconstitutional unless-** (1) the law is necessary to achieve an important government interest, (2) there has been express Congressional approval or (3) the state/local government is a market participant favoring its own citizens.

Dormant Commerce Clause- Law will be upheld unless it places on undue burden on interstate commerce. i.e. it's burdens outweigh the benefits.

Abortion/ Fetus Viability- State cannot place an undue burden on the fundamental right of a woman to reproductive choice prior to fetal viability. The rule is that prior to viability (i.e. late in second trimester), states may not prohibit abortions but a state may regulate so long as the regulation does not create an undue burden on one's ability to get an abortion.

State Taxation of U.S. The rule is that states may not tax federal government activity, i.e. it is unconstitutional to pay a state tax out of the federal treasury. However, a nondiscriminatory state income tax on an employee of the federal government does not impose a burden on the United States.

Congressional Delegation Power- If: 1. Intelligible standards are set; and 2. The power is not uniquely confined to Congress. (i.e. power to impeach/declare wars)

- General rule that prevents Congress from enacting a statute overruling a SCOTUS decision does not apply to Congress enacting statutes under the Commerce Clause

Bill of Attainder: A legislative Act that singles out particular individuals for punishment without a trial.

Equal Protection: Federal- 5th Amend | State- 14th

- Ask: 1) What is the classification? (i.e facial discrimination or facially neutral but discriminatory impact) 2. What level of scrutiny applies?; and 3. Does the particular action meet that level of scrutiny?

Limited Public Forum- is created when a governmental entity could close a location to speech but instead has opened it for speech. (MOST COMMON IN SCHOOLS)

- When a school opens its classrooms for use by student groups, it creates LPF and may not deny access to use that room for students based on the content of their speech

Time, place and Manner restriction: Involves the shifting of time and speech from one time and place to another or to another moment. (If no shifting= direct punishment)

Public Forum Leafletting: Subject to first amendment, because it is expressive activity.

- When expression takes place on Government owned property, government regulation of that expression is asserted under the public forum doctrine.

- Public streets and sidewalks- examples of traditional public forums open to the public for expression
- 'When state tries to regulate expressive activity in a traditional public forum, it is prohibited from doing so based on the expressive activities content unless its regulation is narrowly tailed to achieve a compelling government interest'

Public Schools: Although children in public schools have some first amendment rights, schools have greater leeway to regulate the speech of students and teachers than the state would outside the schools.

- Except: Public school may not force their students to participate in a flat salute ceremony when it offends the political or religious beliefs of the students or their families

Due Process clause- Entitles an individual to notice and a hearing before being deprived of an interest in liberty or property.

- **DOES NOT APPLY TO LEGISLATIVE ACTS (BILL OF ATTAINDER DOES)**
- Would apply to a reform that relieved the prosecution of the burden to prove each and every element of a criminal offense beyond a reasonable doubt.
- Insanity = NOT an element of an offense

State Preventing New political party from appearing on ballot- Would be a freedom of speech issue, but because you are dealing with the state, you would attack the Constitutionality of the act under the 14th Amendment

5th Amendment- Nor shall private property be taken for public use without just compensation

Taking- Permanent physical occupation, even if portion is unused by landowner or is very small.

- **Possessory Taking-** Gov confiscates or physically occupies property
- **Regulatory Taking-** When the Gov regulation leaves no reasonable economically viable use for the property **Factors:** 1. The economic impact of the regulation on the claimant; 2. The extent to which the regulation has interfered with the investment backed expectation; and 3. The character of the Governmental Action
- **Examples of Reg:** Zoning ordinances- Won't be found to be taking when no evidence that suggests prohibition on development will reduce value of lot in question
- , conditions on development- is taking if the burden imposed by the condition is not roughly proportional to the gov justification for regulations
- **If taking not for public use-** GOV MUST GIVE PROPERTY BACK
- **Public Use-** Having a rationally related to a conceivable public purpose
- **Just Compensation-** Measured in terms of loss to the owner (gain to the gov irrelevant)—GOV must pay just compensation even if temporary taking

<u>Restrictions on Development-</u> The rule is that government restrictions on development must be justified by a benefit that is roughly proportionate to the burden imposed by the proposed development or there will be a taking.

<u>10th Amendment Federalism Concepts-</u> Disables Congress from requiring states to enact laws or to administer Federal Law

- **Violated when:** Statute commandeers a city to regulate conduct of others
- **Not violated when:** Regulates city on same terms as other entities engaged in the same conduct

<u>11th Amendment</u>- ' The judicial power of the US shall not be construed to extend to any suit in law or in equity commenced or prosecuted against one of the United States by Citizens of another state or by citizens or subjects of any foreign state'

Prevents award of monetary relief from states treasury

<u>11th doesn't bar-</u> Suit against state officials which $ paid would be from officials pocket.

- 11th doesn't bar the Federal Court from granting an injunction even if it would cause a state to lose profits by it being granting
- **Waiving Immunity-** State consents to suit in Federal Court. How? → Must specifically state the intention to subject itself to suit in Federal Court.
- **EX:** Ineffective waiver of immunity- State statute authorizes state to be sued in any court of competent jurisdiction.

<u>Ex Parte young-</u> Can enjoin enforcement of a unconstitutional law that is in violation of Federal Law on a state official. (11th won't bar)

- Why? Can't claim he is part of state

<u>Congress Abrogation of State 11th Amendment Immunity-</u>Can only do so if acting under S5 power and not any other authority.

- Law must expressly do so in its text
- Congress authorizing suits against states for patent infringement- exceeds the scope of Congress S5 authority

<u>Title II-</u> States may be sued for discriminating against individuals with disability. (i.e. access to Courthouses)

<u>Criminal Law/ Procedure</u>

<u>Fourth Amendment-</u> Prohibits unreasonable searches and seizures. (i.e. those involving state action which intrude upon an individual's reasonable expectation of privacy).

<u>Automatic Standing-</u> When a search takes place in a suspect's home, in a place owned by the suspect or where the suspect is an overnight guest of the owner of the place. (if owner consent to search then no standing for overnight guest)

<u>Plain view-</u> Can't object if officer observes illegal actions from a neighbors property

<u>Involuntary Manslaughter-</u>To be guilty, a person must cause the death of another human being by conduct that creates an unreasonable high risk of death or serious bodily injury. The precise mens rea requirement will vary from jurisdiction to jurisdiction.

- <u>Modern/Majority view-</u> D must have acted recklessly to be convicted. (i..e must have been aware of high risk of death/SBI his conduct created)
- <u>Mens Rea-</u> Of reckless/or gross negligence. If fact finder accepts D did not consciously disregard an unreasonable risk of death/sbi- not guilty in a jurisdiction that requires recklessness for the crime
- <u>Recklessness-</u> Conscious disregard of a known risk
- <u>Causation-</u> Requires a showing of both causation in fact & proximate cause

<u>Common law murder</u> is the intentional killing of a person with malice aforethought. Malice aforethought requires that the killing be committed with one of the following states of mind: (1) intent to kill, (2) intent to commit great bodily injury, (3) wanton and willful disregard of human life or (4) intent to commit felony (i.e. felony murder rule).

<u>Second Degree Murder-</u>

- Example- Playing Russian Roulette- 2nd degree murder because requirements of a subjective awareness of an unjustified high risk to human life

<u>LaFave Intent-</u> One intends certain consequences when he desires that his acts cause those consequence or knows that those consequences are substantially certain to result from his acts.

- **Intent to kill-** Which a person intended to kill another human being
- **False pretenses-** Intended to deceive the victim
- **Burglary-** Intentionally engaged in the conduct of B&E
- **Larceny-** Thief intentionally engages in the taking/carrying away of property

<u>MPC</u>

- **Knowingly-** If he is aware that it is practically certain that his conduct will cause such a result
- **Purposely-** It is his conscious object to cause such a result

<u>Depraved Heart Murder-</u> Even if lack of intent to kill, where there is conduct that 'creates such a high risk of death and was so devoid of social utility'

<u>Accomplice liability-</u>the scope of liability includes liability for the intended crime and all other foreseeable crimes committed by the principals.

<u>Felony Murder Rule-</u> Will apply during the commission of an inherently dangerous felony. i.e. robbing a house and homeowner has a heart attack.

<u>Self-defense-</u> Permits use of force reasonably believes necessary given threat posed by the attacker.

<u>Self-Defense Deadly Force-</u> victim may use deadly force if victim is not at fault and is confront with unlawful force and reasonably believes she is facing imminent threat of death or great bodily harm.

- **Majority Rule-** No duty to retreat
- **Minority Rule-** No duty to retreat if the attack takes place in victims home.

<u>Conspiracy</u>

- **Common law elements:** 1. An agreement between 2 or more persons (act) and; 2. An intent to achieve a certain objective. (doing of either a lawful or unlawful act by unlawful means)
- **Overt Act-** A step towards the execution of the conspiracy. An act that tends to carry out the conspiracy. An act that effects the object of the conspiracy or a step in preparation for the effecting the objective. Virtually any act will satisfy. (EX: making a phone call/ attending a lawful meeting/ giving co-conspirator $/ meeting with a lawyer)
- - Only needs to be done by one of the conspirators
- **If Defendant charged and other only conspiracy member acquitted/ or only member who performed overt act acquitted-** all other members must also be acquitted
- **Conspiracy w/ Multiple objectives-** Guilty of only one conspiracy as long as the multiple crimes are the object of the same agreement or continuous conspiratol relationship
  - **Common Law-** 2 persons required | **MPC-** Only 1 (unilateral)
  - **Agreement-** Need not be explicit, can be shown from meeting of the minds and possible for various parties to be parties to a single conspiracy even if they don't know each other
  - **Aiding a conspiracy w/ knowledge of its purpose=** sufficient to make one a party to a conspiracy
- RE: Statutory rape Person (over 18) cannot be convicted if statute was written to protect a certain class of people, because a person within that class cannot be found guilty of the crime and, therefore, cannot be guilty of a conspiracy to commit that crime
- **Conspiracy terminates when:** either: 1. The crimes that are it's object are committed; or 2. It is abandoned by the D and by those with whom he conspired. If an individual abandons= terminated only as to him if/when he advises those with whom he conspired of the abandonment or informs the authorities of the conspiracy and his particular involvement.
- **Mental state:** Must in some sense promote the venture himself/ make it his own or have a stake in the outcome

Attempt-

- **Legal Impossibility-** Is a defense. If what D set out to do is not criminal then he is not guilty of attempt
- **Examples:** D attempted to take deer out of season when the deer he shot was stuffed. D intended to bribe juror but person bribed not a juror.
- **Factual Impossibility-** Is not a defense. Where the intended substantive crime is impossible merely because of some physical impossibility unknown to the D.
- **Examples:** D attempts to kill w/ false bomb. D attempts to sell cocaine that was flour

Custody- Suspect does not reasonably believe that she is free to terminate the encounter with the Government.

Interrogation- Conduct that the police know or should have known was likely to elicit an incriminating response from the suspect.

Grand Jury Witness- No right to have counsel inside the Grand Jury room and EXCLUSIONARY RULE DOESN"T APPLY TO GRAND JURY PROCEEDINGS EVER

Jury Trial Applies- Crime punishable by more than 6 months in prison.

Right to Counsel- Applies when misdemeanors with possible jail sentence. Applies to suspended sentence too.

6th Amendment violation- When a sentence enhancement is created by any fact that increases the penalty for a crime beyond the statutorily prescribed period, that fact must be submitted to jury and proven BARD.

5th Amendment Double Jeopardy- Provides that a person shall not be twice put in jeopardy for the same offense.

- **Lesser included offense:** If the elements of the lesser charge are not wholly contained in the greater charge, then convicting D of both crimes would not violate the double jeopardy clause even when the two offenses occurred at the same time and ae arguably part of the same transaction.

Use/Derivative Use- Sufficiently protects privilege against self-incrimination

Wharton's Rule- an agreement by 2 people to commit a crime cannot be prosecuted as a conspiracy if the substantive crime involved requires at least 2 people to commit.

Accomplice Liability: 1. The intent to assist the primary party; and 2. The intent that the primary party commit the offense charged

- Even a small amount of assistance can suffice to create liability. Mere presence is not enough

Terry Stop- The rule is that an officer who has an articulable and reasonable suspicion to believe that a person was, is or will be, engaged in criminal activity may stop the suspect and conduct a warrantless frisk for weapon

Contracts/ Article II

Sale of Goods- Contracts for the sale of goods are governed by Article 2 of the Uniform Commercial Code.

Revocation of Offer-The rule is that the offeree must have notice of a revocation of an offer in order for the revocation to be effective. The act of making multiple offers does not by itself revoke earlier offers and if one offeree accepts, the offeror must notify every other offeree to effectively revoke the other offers

Anticipatory Repudiation- the rule is that where a party unambiguously states by words or conduct to the other party, before the time for performance has arisen, that she will not perform or that she is unable to perform, the other party is entitled to treat that as an anticipatory repudiation that generally excuses performance by the non-repudiating party. A breach of contract occurs when a party to the contract does not perform after performance comes due

Goods- Those movable things identifiable at the time of contract. (Tangible personal property)

Express Contract- A contract formed expressly by language, either written or oral.

Implied Contract- Contract formed by conduct. (i.e. assent by means other than written or oral language).

Offer Invites Acceptance by Performance- The offerees beginning of performance creates an option contract which precludes the offeror from revoking the offer

UCC 2-204(1)- Provides that a contract for a sale of goods may be made in any manner sufficient to show agreement, including conduct by both parties which recognizes the existence of a K.

UCC 2-201(1)- A contract for the sale of goods for the price of $500 or more is not enforceable by way of action or defense unless there is some writing sufficient to indicate that a K for sale has been made between the parties and is signed by the party against whom enforcement is sought.

- **2-201(C)(3)**- a contract that does not satisfy the S.O.F is nonetheless enforceable as to "goods for which payment has been made & accepted or which have been received and accepted"

Signed- Includes using any symbol executed or adopted with present intention to adopt or accept a writing.

- Letterhead—can be a signing if it was used with a present to adopt/accept the document

<u>Merchant-</u> Means a person who deals in goods of the kind or otherwise by his occupation holds himself out as having knowledge or skill peculiar to the practice involved in the transaction or to whom such knowledge may be attributable by his employment of an agent.

- **Between merchants:** Means in any transaction in which both parties are charged with the knowledge or skill of merchants.
- <u>Merchants EX:</u> Transaction involves knife manufacturer and chef → '*The manufacturer deals in goods of that kind at issue and the chefs occupation is such that he would have the knowledge or skills peculiar to the goods involved in the transaction*'

<u>Express Contractual Condition-</u> Language in a K that states something must occur before someones performance is due.

- Who can waive express condition? The party protected by it
- If condition not satisfied- non performance is excused.

<u>Doctrine of Prevention-</u> requires that a party refrain from conduct that prevents or hinders the occurrence of a condition.

<u>Economic Duress-</u> Applies to CL Ks and UCC Art II—'A contract is voidable on the ground of economic duress by threat when it is established that a party's manifestation of assent is induced by an improper threat that leaves the party no reasonable alternative'

- **Elements:** 1. A threat was made; 2. The threat was improper or wrongful; 3. The threat induced the others manifestation of assent to a modification; and 4. The threat was sufficiently grave to justify the others assent
- **Mere threat to breach-** in and of itself, insufficient

<u>Accord/Satisfaction-</u> An accord is an agreement to accept a different performance in satisfaction of the existing obligation. However, the rule is that if a debt is due and undisputed, part payment is not new consideration for settlement or release.

<u>UCC 2-311-</u> Selection of Goods- imposes a duty on buyer to cooperate by specifying the goods when the K fails to so provide. A seller can treat the buyers failure to specify as a breach by failure to accept the contracted for goods. <u>Only-</u> if the buyers failure to specify materially impairs the sellers performance.

<u>If seller forms K by promising to ship and then seller ships non-conforming Goods w/ Notice of Accommodation-</u> Would be a breach of K allowing the buyer to accept or reject the non-conforming goods and recover damages in either event.

- Why? → K was formed at moment seller made promise to ship (sent via letter)

<u>Adequate Assurances-</u> Where one party has reasonable grounds for insecurity with respect to the others performance, they can demand seeking assurance of the others performance under the K and failure of the other to provide such assurance within a reasonable time will constitute repudiation of the K.

- Contract parties are entitled to expect due performance of K obligation and are entitled to take reasonable steps to protect that expectation
- When reasonable grounds for insecurity arises with respect to the performance of either party, the other may in writing, demand adequate assurance of due performance
- **After receipt-** failure to provide within a reasonable time, not exceeding 30 days, assurance of due performance, is a repudiation of the K.
- **Free to retract repudiation-** until other party cancels the contract, materially changes his position or otherwise indicates he considers the repudiation final.

Unequivocal Refusal to Perform- The rule is that where a party unambiguously states by words or conduct to the other party, before the time for performance has arisen, that she will not perform or that she is unable to perform, the other party is entitled to treat that as an anticipatory repudiation that generally excuses performance by the non-repudiating party.

Parol Evidence Rule- states that no prior expressions (written or oral) or contemporaneous oral statements are admissible to contradict the final integration between the parties. For the parol evidence rule to apply, there must be an integration, i.e. a written agreement intended to be the final contract between the parties. Integration can be complete or partial. While parol evidence is inadmissible to contradict, it is admissible for both partial or complete integrations (1) to show a clerical error, (2) to show a defense to contract formation, (3) to clarify ambiguous terms, (4) to show a consistent collateral contract and (5) to show the existence of a condition precedent.

When a seller has an action for the contract price- 1. When the buyer has accepted the goods; 2. The goods are lost/damaged within a commercially reasonable time after the R.O.L has passed to the buyer; or 3. The seller is unable to resell the goods after reasonable efforts.

Simultaneous Contract- Each party must first tender performance before a duty will be imposed on other party to perform. i.e. deliver 25 on 3/1 and 25 on 4/1→ Seller would have no duty to deliver on 3/1 unless buyer tenders contract price for the 25 sets on that date.

Installment Sales Contract- A contract that requires or authorized multiple shipments in installments with multiple payments. a buyer can reject an installment delivery only if the nonconformity substantially impairs the value of that installment and it cannot be cured.

Shipment Contract- Risk of loss passes from seller-buyer when the seller duly delivers goods to the 3rd party carrier

Conversion after rightfully rejected goods- If buyer sells goods after rejecting, conduct in selling would be wrongful against seller and would constitute a conversion.

- **Remedy for Conversion-** Fair market value of the goods at the time of the conversion. EX: If original K was for 100k and the buyer who rejects sells for 120K—liable to seller for 120k

Consequential Damages- to be recoverable these damages must have arose naturally from the breach and they must have been reasonably foreseeable at the time of contract formation.

Pre-Existing Duty Rule- When there is a compromise of a claim disputed in Good Faith. Applies even if it later becomes apparent that the reason for disputing the claim was invalid.

UCC 2-613- Provides that when Good identified at the time K was made are totally destroyed before the risk of loss has passed to the buyer and without the fault of either party, the K is avoided and each party is relieved of its respective obligation to perform

Parol Evidence- allows admissibility of extrinsic evidence to establish that a parties performance under a written K was subject to an oral condition.

Course of Performance- Parties to an agreement know best what they meant and that action is often the strongest evidence of their meaning.

- When it is unreasonable to interpret the K in accordance with the course of performance- conduct of parties may be evidence of an agreed modification or a waiver by one party

Technical Terms- Technical terms are often misused that a technical term was used in a non-technical sense.

- Parties to an agreement often use the vocabulary of a particular place, vocation or trade in which new words are coined and common words are assigned new meaning.

General Usage- In the absence of some contrary indication, English words are read as having he meaning given to them by general usage, if there is one.

- Applies in the absence of some contrary indication

Interpretation of the whole- Meaning is inevitably dependent on context. i.e. a word changes meaning when it becomes part of a sentence and a sentence changes meaning when it becomes of a paragraph, etc etc.

Principal Purpose- Purpose of parties K isn't always identical. But up to a point they commonly join in a common purpose of attaining a specific factual or legal result which regards as necessary to the attainment of his ultimate purpose.

Circumstances- Meaning of words/conduct is dependent on their circumstances. In interpreting the words/conduct of parties to a K, a court seeks to put itself in the position they occupied at the time K was made. When the parties have adopted a writing as a final expression of their agreement, interpretation is directed at the meaning of that writing in light of the circumstances. Includes the entire situation as it appeared to the parties.

Article III

Article3

- Will be check or promissory note

Have to give def if negotiability – this transaction will be governed by Uniform Commercial Code Article 3 negotiable instrument.

- Note or check is negotiable – **negotiability** – unconditional promise to pay a sum certain on demand or at a definite time payable to order or bearer.

Signed by maker of note, drawer from bank …

- Always will have a **HIDC** or someone almost there. – takes the note or check in good faith for value without any notice of claims or defenses against it.

#1 claim usually is that was due by the date, note has become due. If I am a HIDC and I find out note was later stolen or altered.

- Go for payment of note and they have a defense against a HIDC

Real defenses can be raised against a HIDC

- Signed his name forgery by trick.
- Breach of K, 93A,
- If can't get money on note must for value –

Person who transferred to me can also sue on warranties ---

Identify that transaction is governed by Article 3 of Uniform Commercial code.

→ Talk about negotiability and list the elements
You will have a holder or almost holder. – just need to identify.

→ Likely to test on real defenses and warranties
Sometimes **conversion** – stealing check

→ Someone adds a 0- might also be misrep in tort

- Real challenging shitshow of question lands on question 8.

- Sue breach in contract and can also sue to enforce the note

- Without recourse doesn't excuse you in warranties, may excuse for payment to immediate transfers. But doesn't shield from breach of warranty claims under Article 3.

- Best defenses are breach of warranties under article 3 &

- Breach of K under common law contract principals.

- **Duty of bailor** – hold in care and not to damage.

- Unique – equity as remedy – damages at law wont help.

- Article 3 steps and negotiable elements gov by UCC article 3 negotiable instruments

- Constructive trust -→ anything over the amount of fair market value

- Think equity and specific performance.

Evidence

Hearsay: Statement that: 1) The declarant does not make while testifying at the current trial or hearing; and 2) A party offers as evidence to prove the truth of the matter asserted in the statement.
- **Statement:** A persons oral assertion, written assertions or nonverbal conduct if the person intended it as an assertion
- **Assertion:** (NON HEARSAY) Simply means to say that something is so

Admission of party opponent: both substantive/impeachment

Attorney Client Privilege- Applies only to confidential communications made for the purpose of facilitating legal representation of the client. (doesn't cover fee arrangement/payment)
- Crime fraud exception: if the communication is made to further what client knew or should have known to be a crime or fraud then ACP doesn't apply.

<u>Present Sense Impression-</u> statement that describes an event or condition made while the declarant was perceiving it or immediately thereafter.

<u>Excited Utterance:</u> No requirement be present to testify

<u>Past Recollection Recorded-</u> A record concerning a matter about which a witness once had knowledge made while the matter was fresh in the witnesses memory and reflects that knowledge correctly, but now has insufficient recollection to testify fully & accurately.

<u>Refreshing Recollection:</u> When an otherwise inadmissible document is shown to a witness to refresh his recollection, witness must read it to himself. It is improper to allow such a document to be read aloud to the jury and it may be admitted as an exhibit only if offered by the lawyer who was not used the exhibit to refresh the recollection of the witness.

<u>404(A)</u> Evidence of a persons character or a trait of character is not admissible for the purpose of proving conformity therewith on a particular occasion.

<u>Prior Inconsistent Statement-</u> Non-hearsay- To be admissible to prove the truth of the matter asserted, the prior statement must have been under oath, subject to pain and penalty of perjury at a trial, hearing or in a deposition.

<u>406-</u> Habit evidence is admissible to prove that a person acted in conformity with that habit. This is true even if the only evidence of habit is the persons own testimony.

<u>608(B)</u> Allows witnesses to be cross-examine about specific instance of prior non-convictions of misconduct probative of untruthfulness, in order to attack the witnesses character for truthfulness
- Expressly prohibits the use of extrinsic evidence to impeach a witnesses character for truthfulness. Specific instances of conduct for the purpose of attacking or supporting the witnesses character for truthfulness may not be proved by extrinsic evidence. Thus, is W questions about an alleged lie and he refuses to admit to lying, he may not be contradicted by extrinsic evidence.
- False statement (EX expert lies about degree) Probative of untruthfulness because grossly misrepresents academic credential.

- **Extrinsic evidence-** Court doesn't have any discretion to admit. Creates risk of confusing jurors

407- When measures are taken that would have made an earlier injury or harm less likely to occur; evidence of the subsequent measures is not admissible to prove negligence. Even when relevant still excluded based on a policy of encouraging people to take, or at least not discouraging them from taking steps in furtherance of added safety

408- Bars evidence that a party furnished or promises/offered as valuable consideration in attempting to compromise the disputed claim. Offers to settle disputed claims are excluded based on the promotion of public policy favoring the compromise and settlement of disputes.

409 Offers to pay medical bills- Precludes admission of evidence of furnishing, promising to pay or offering to pay medical expenses resulting from an injury to prove liability for that injury. Does not require that statement be made in response to a disputed claim.

Slander Character Evidence: relevant to prove: 1. Whether P has a certain character; and 2. The extent of damages

911 Call Transcript analysis: Either 1. Present Sense Impression; 2. Excited Utterance; 3. Statement made for purposes of medical diagnosis or treatment. And describing medical history, past or present symptoms or sensations, their inception or general cause (i.e. if dispatcher is asking questions and caller statement relevant to current medical condition and fact that caller likely needs treatment)

701 Witness who not testifying as an expert, may offer an opinion only if: 1. The opinion is rationally based on w's perception of what happened; 2. The opinion helps determine a fact in issue; and 3. The opinion is not based on scientific, technical or other specialized knowledge

Psychotherapist duty to warn: Has a duty to warn a reasonably identifiable individual against whom her patient has made credible threats but has no duty to warn any individual who is a member of an indeterminate class against whom the patient has made threats
- Special relationship between psychotherapist and paint justifies imposition of a duty to warn persons threatened by the patient

- **Duty imposed where either:** 1. When therapist believed patient posed real threat to specific victim; or 2. When therapist negligently failed to take threat seriously

Standard of review of alleged error in evidentiary hearing- Abuse of discretion

Made in the USA
Middletown, DE
03 January 2020

82474006R00028